STAY
CONNECTED

Dedication

This book is dedicated to everyone who has played a vital role in helping me to grow and bloom into the woman I am today. I want to thank my parents, my children, family, friends, spiritual leaders, co-workers, and my ex-husband. Thank you all for sowing seeds into my life. We all will reap the harvest together, in Jesus's mighty name. Amen.

STAY CONNECTED

DEIRDRE JOYNER

Editor
Kendra Friendly

ASA PUBLISHING CORPORATION
AN INNOVATIVE OUTSOURCE BOOK PUBLISHING HYBRID

ASA Publishing Corporation
1285 N. Telegraph Rd., PMB #376, Monroe, Michigan 48162
An Accredited Publishing House with the BBB
www.asapublishingcorporation.com

All Rights Reserved. No part of this publication may be reproduced, stored in a retrieval system or transmitted in any form or by any means electronic, mechanical, photocopying, recording or otherwise, without the prior written permission of the publisher. Author/writer rights to "Freedom of Speech" protected by and with the "1st Amendment" of the Constitution of the United States of America. This is a work of non-fiction; Christian education. Any resemblance to actual events, locales, person living or deceased that is not related to the author's literacy is entirely coincidental.

With this title/copyright page, the reader is notified that the publisher does not assume, and expressly disclaims any obligation to obtain and/or include any other information other than that provided by the author except with permission. Any belief system, promotional motivations, including but not limited to the use of non-fictional/fictional characters and/or characteristics of this book, are within the boundaries of the author's own creativity in order to reflect the nature and concept of the book. Unless otherwise indicated, all scripture quotations are Christian biblically based.

Any and all vending sales and distribution not permitted without full book cover and this copyright page.

Copyrights©2021 Deirdre Joyner, All Rights Reserved
Book Title: Stay Connected
Date Published: 02.23.2021 / Edition 1 *Trade Paperback*
Book ID: ASAPCID2380824
ISBN: 978-1-946746-76-4
Library of Congress Cataloging-in-Publication Data
    This book was published in the United States of America.
    Great State of Michigan

Acknowledgments

I would like to take this time to thank my parents, Eddie B. Jones, and Mary K. Jones, for laying a strong foundation for me to stand on. Proverbs 22:6 says, "Train up a child in the way he should go; and when he is old, he will not depart from it." Momma and Dad, you have done just that, and I am extremely grateful. Thank you for giving me a good upbringing with love, structure, morals, values, curfews, guidance, and strict rules. I didn't always understand it or like it! I even had my share of fighting against it, but today I see that I was truly blessed. Thank you; job well done!

To my daughters, Shaniece and T'Airra, I am so thankful for you both. You've been by my side ever since I was a youngster trying to figure it all out. We've weathered many storms together and celebrated many triumphs. You two are the primary reasons why I decided to seek God and change my life. I wanted to rid my heart, mind, and life of any and everything that was hindering me from being the best mother that I could be. You two were my silent strength in fighting some of the most challenging battles in my life. I fought boldly and courageously because I wanted to be an example of what a good Godly woman and mother looked like. It took a while, but I thank God that you were able to see your mother's transformation in Christ. You two are all grown up with children of your own, and I still make decisions based on the fact that I have two daughters looking up to me. I pray that I have given you both useful tools on what you should and should not do as a woman and a mother. If I haven't taught you ladies anything else, I pray that I've shown both of you that life is much better when God is the center. No matter where you are and no matter what you're going through, please don't ever give up on God, because He will never give up on you! Love Momma!

I cannot and will not leave out Mr. Jeffrey Joyner. We spent almost twenty years of our lives together. Although we are no longer together as husband and wife, I cannot deny the fact that you helped me to become better. I wanted to become a better wife, mother, and woman for you and our family. This desire led me to dig deeper into forming a relationship with God. I spent many days praying and fasting on behalf of our marriage and our family! Although the marriage ended, my gratefulness for you will live on forever. I thank you for giving me a better prayer life. I thank you for being a great father to the girls. I thank you for sharing your wisdom and intelligence with us. I especially thank you for helping me to get through college math and for teaching me how to write an *A* paper in half the time. Thank you for every time you went to Kinko's in the middle of the night and typed my papers. Who knew that you were grooming a future author! Lord knows I never would've made it without you! Jeff, there's no doubt in my mind that our relationship, marriage, and divorce has been instrumental in grooming me into the woman I am today. I truly appreciate you and all your sacrifices over the years. Thank you, and may God return it all right back to ya!

I would also love to give one big shout-out to my siblings, especially Kathrine, Kelly, and Ebony. Kat, I love the fact that you are the meekest person I know. I'm so thankful that I can pour my heart out to you without any judgment in return. You've kept many of my secrets and I love you for that! Thanks for every conversation. We laugh; we cry; we pray and repeat. You are my dog bootie for life! Sorry readers, it's personal.

To the schoolgirl, Kelly. I'm so proud of you for going after and accomplishing all of your goals. I love that we can talk about the kingdom of God together. I am humbled at the fact that you include me in your homework assignments by sharing your answers and asking my opinion. It brought me such joy when you wrote a paper on my spiritual transformation. Thank you for seeing me as worthy, and thanks for taking an interest in my spiritual journey. I look forward to doing God's work with you in the near future.

Ebony, you were right there with me when I was in the world. You've witnessed me at my worst, and I thank God that I got a chance to "get it right," to be a better example of a big sister. This is the life, Sis. All of that craziness was just a road to this journey. God bless you and may God show you great success in all that you do!

Thanks to each one of you for supporting my last project. I love you all, and I am grateful to call you my baby sisters.

Brenda L. Wiggins, my special friend in Christ; the big sister I never had. Words cannot explain the appreciation, love, respect, and adoration that I have for you! Our friendship has been a blessing for almost two decades. You helped me maneuver through some critical times as a woman, mother, and wife. Thanks for listening, advising, and praying. May God's favor rain on you, Brittany, Ni, and your entire family for generations yet to come. Love D.

I cannot forget about my former co-worker and my dear friend, Ms. Janice Gayle. Thank you for all your support and for propelling me into a whole new life and career. This new venture has been amazing! Thank you for believing in me. You saw things in me that I didn't see in myself. Thank you for all your prayers. Thanks for sharing years of wisdom and life lessons with me. It's greatly appreciated! I'm so glad that our paths had crossed again. I'm blessed to have you! I love you Sista!

Evangelist Willie Dillard, you are an amazing friend and mentor. I love you to pieces and thank God for you, our friendship, and your ministry. You have been a blessing to not only me but to my entire family. Thank you for every time you prayed and laid hands over me. May God return it all to you in money and in what money cannot buy! Peace, love, joy, healing, deliverance, good health, wisdom. . .

Last but not least, my deepest appreciation goes to Mr. Hill and the amazing staff at ASA Publishing. I am so thankful for your creative and editorial gifts that make my work better. Thank you, Mr. Hill, for giving me an affordable platform that allows me to reach individuals for the Kingdom of God. May God continue to bless the work of your hands. Thank you and God Bless you all!

I apologize to anyone who was not mentioned. I have numerous family and friends, so it would be almost impossible to address everyone. I love you all; please don't take it personally.

Thank you

Deirdre

Table of Contents

Dedication ....
Acknowledgments 1

Introductory 1
   Reason 1 13
   Reason 2 29
   Reason 3 41
      Salvation 46
      Freedom/Forgiveness 46
      Protection 49
      Deliverance 52
      Peace 55
      Healing 58
      Provision 60
      Grace/Mercy 64
      Joy 67

Seven Simple Disciplines 73
   Go to Church 75
   Prioritize Your Day 76
   Give 79
   Serve 81

Pray 83

Be Obedient 89

Be Thankful 94

STAY CONNECTED

DEIRDRE JOYNER

Introductory

In April 2019, I asked my readers to Make God a Habit via a twenty-one-day challenge. The sole purpose of that book was to help people either connect to God, reconnect with Him, or strengthen the connection that had already existed.

It was my sincere prayer that people would've continued spending time with God after the twenty-one days had concluded. I was hoping that people would've made it a priority to seek God each day. I wanted all of my readers to crave God, to thirst, and hunger for Him on a much deeper and intimate level. I am not sure how many people I reached through that book, and I am not sure how many people actually did Make God A Habit. Truthfully, my job would've been accomplished if just one person read the book and continued their journey with God.

However, I do wish that I could've reached more people, millions perhaps. I don't say this just for the sake of notoriety, book sales, or money. More importantly, I say it because of the times we are living in today. We're currently living in unprecedented times.

COVID-19, a very contagious and fatal disease caused by a novel coronavirus, has caused a global pandemic dating back to approximately March of 2020. The respiratory disease rapidly spread affecting people of approximately 151 countries. Many of the infected displayed symptoms of fever, cough, shortness of breath, fatigue, and body aches. The list of symptoms increased as researchers and medical officials found out more about the disease.

The numbers for confirmed cases and deaths continued to rise daily, radically altering the lifestyles of the American people. The rapid spread of the disease, the shelter in place orders, social distancing, the loss of jobs, the rising unemployment rates, the lack of work hours, the lack of food supply, and the lack of household essentials caused panic, fear, depression, and anxiety.

The United States government stepped in to provide some financial relief for qualifying Americans by passing The Economic Impact Payment Act. Since then, there have been discussions that the government will provide more economic relief. Hopefully, there is more help on the way for the American people, but if not, I want everyone to know where their help comes from. Know that, "God will meet all your needs according to the riches of His glory in Christ

Jesus." Phil. 4:19 (NIV).

That is why I wish that more people would've read and taken heed to Make God A Habit: A 21-Day Challenge. More people would've been spiritually equipped to weather the storms of COVID-19. I wish that more people knew that they could live during a global pandemic and still have perfect peace, no fear, or anxiety. If more people knew this and lived by this fact, we would not have seen the initial public response to the disease.

My goodness, people were fighting while shopping for groceries and household cleaning products. There were arguments and shoving matches over toilet paper! People were greedy and selfish by filling their carts up with more food and supplies than they could use in a two to three-month period. Out of fear and panic, people had forgotten, or maybe some never knew that according to Psalm 23:1, the Lord is our shepherd and we shall not want. If you were one of the people who were panicking and facing anxiety, please find peace in knowing that 1 Peter 5:7 says that you can cast all your concerns, cares, worries, and fears on God because He cares for you.

Then, as our nation began to transition back to normal, we experienced another pandemic—police brutality against African Americans, and especially black men. The horrific and unjust murder of George Floyd by a Minneapolis police officer stirred up worldwide protests and riots. People of all races came together again to take a stand against the systemic racism that blacks have endured by police and the criminal justice system.

Since Mr. Floyd's death, the outrage and demand for change have produced some small results across the country within the criminal justice system and police departments. We have a long way to go, and the only way we're going to get there is with God's help. Yes, keep marching and protesting, but in the midst, we have to take the time to ask God to search the hearts of all people. As a whole, this country has a serious heart condition and several of us are in need of a heart transplant. Ezekiel 36:26 records that God will take away the heart of stone and replace it with a heart of flesh and a new spirit.

We need this transformation to take place in our homes, jobs, schools, and with our leaders and politicians on a national, state, and local level. We cannot fight spiritual warfare by protesting or rioting and expect effective positive change. We have to do it all. We have to fight the battle in the spirit and allow God to lead us to the right people and places. If we include Him first, the battle is already won, so we must show up to receive the victory in Jesus's mighty name.

There is nothing that we are facing or will ever face as individuals or a nation that God cannot and will not work out for our good. We have to call it out in prayer and then surrender it to Him so that He can do with it as He sees fit, in His way and time. On that note, I would like to stop and take the time to pray right now.

Heavenly Father, we humbly come before you with thanksgiving in our hearts. Father God, we thank you for this day; we thank you for this very moment; we thank you that we have breath in our bodies, and we thank you Lord that we can see, hear, taste, and smell. We thank you for your presence, provision, and power. Lord, we know that there is nothing that is too big for you! You are the God over COVID-19, and you are the God over every sickness that has ever fallen on your people. Lord, we also know that you are the God over unemployment, lack, poverty, racism, and oppression. Lord, you delivered the children of Israel from bondage, oppression, and unfair treatment. Lord, we believe that you will do the same for us today! As we seek you, Lord show us how to work with you for the equality of all people. Knowing that you are the God over it all allows us to rest in you fully, Lord. We give you every concern right now; we give you anxiety, fear, worry, depression, anger, hate, revenge, unfair laws, and the crooked hearts of those behind them. Lord, make the crooked places straight! Lord, we also give you the grocery list, the diagnosis, and the bills. Lord, we give it all to you because we know that you are able! Your well never runs dry and we are so very thankful that we are your children with an inheritance of overflow. We receive the overflow right now in

Jesus's name. Amen.

As I mentioned earlier, I asked my readers last year to make God a habit. The follow-up to that is, now I'm asking you to stay connected. The purpose of this book is to get my readers to stay connected to the source and get closer to Him on an intimate level. It is my prayer that I can connect the point and purposes of both books. As well as produce transforming revelation and life-changing decisions that will glorify God as He brings you from where you are in Him to where He wants you to be. Brothers and sisters, it is time to take our salvation more seriously. It is not the time to only be a believer, but rather it's time to be committed Christians that are sold out for the plans and purposes of God!

For the sake of understanding, in this book, I have outlined the reasons we should all stay connected to God, and I have also included a list of disciplined actions that explains what to do to stay connected. Please know that the whys and hows that I present are what I know to be accurate and truthful based on reading, studying, and my experiences. Please do not limit your knowledge to my list because this is just a starting point. In time, you may add to the list or create your own. It is my prayer that the message will be accepted with both open minds and hearts. Heavenly Father, I ask for your presence during the delivery of these words you have given me to say. May each reader of this book be blessed in a mighty way. Thank you in Jesus's name. Amen.

There are many reasons why we should stay connected to God. I've summed them up into three categories. The first discusses that we were created to be in a relationship with our Heavenly Father. The second describes how God desires for us to be in a relationship with Him, and the third details how life is so much better when we're connected. These are the three profound reasons we should stay connected to God. I will examine each one of them in more detail.

Reason 1

We were created to be in a relationship with God, our Heavenly Father

Reason 1

We were created to be in a relationship with God, our Heavenly Father.

No matter how good you think your life is, it is not living if it is not a life lived with God or for him. You are merely existing if you are not in an intimate relationship with God. If you want a life beyond emptiness and dissatisfaction, it must be a life connected to God. I'm not talking about being a believer or being a person who prays when times get rough for you or your loved ones. I am not talking about being a churchgoer either. What I am talking about is being in love with God and being best friends with Him because it is not enough to be just an associate. It is important that every man, woman, and child get to know God, our Heavenly Father, for themselves. The sooner, the better, but better late than never.

Let me share a few facts with you to present my point practically. I think it's safe to say that many of us either know someone who grew up without their earthly father in their lives, or you are that someone. Unfortunately, the fatherless household trend has become a national crisis. According to the article, "The Proof Is In: Father Absence Harms Children," the United States Census Bureau reported in 2019 that one in four children, which is approximately 18.3 million children, lived without a father in the home.[1] This astronomical figure of missing fathers represent kids who did not have a biological father, a stepdad, or an adoptive father available to them on a 24/7 basis.

This national crisis contributes to numerous social and behavioral issues. This article stated that children in fatherless homes are more likely to experience behavioral issues, abuse, experiment with drugs and alcohol, and go to prison. These children are also two times

---

[1] National Fatherhood Initiative, "The Proof Is In: Father Absence Harms Children, (2020), https://www.fatherhood.org/father-absence-statistic.

more likely to suffer obesity and four times more likely to experience poverty. Lastly, girls without full-time dads are seven times more likely to become teen moms.[1]

These statistics are alarming and heartbreaking! However, they do not determine the outcome for every fatherless child. The devil is a liar! There is always hope for those who believe! I'm just presenting the research for the sake of building a foundation to deliver a point. We cannot deny that statistically fatherless children face grim futures. The facts are there, and most of us have personally witnessed and or lived out the trials and tribulations that come with raising children without a father.

So, I guess it's safe to say that we all agree on the fact that children need their fathers. Life is better with a father! Don't get me wrong; I am aware that many fathers are abusive, negative, and irresponsible. I am not talking about those types of fathers. I am talking about the benefits of positive and healthy fathering.

Well, it's no different from the kingdom of God because we need our Heavenly Father! When we try to maneuver through life without our Heavenly Father's presence, guidance, provision, instruction, and protection, we face some grim futures and will travel down some dark and dangerous roads.

As mentioned previously, fatherless children are more susceptible to a life of crime, drugs, and alcohol, which is usually brought on by low self-esteem. Not having a sense of belonging or knowing who they are could lead to a lifestyle of poor decisions and self-destruction. They are trying to fill a void designed for their father. The relationship between father and child is undeniably crucial for a productive life mentally, emotionally, spiritually, financially, and even physically. You will be a better you!

Once again, It's the same with the kingdom of God; we need our Heavenly Father. My life was a mess before I accepted Christ as my personal Lord and Savior. Bad decisions, dating, and hanging out with the wrong people damaged my soul and destroyed my self-esteem. At times I became very depressed and was often prescribed anti-depressants, which I refused to take. If it had not been for God watching over me, I would not be here today! I would've lost my mind and/or my life.

Not knowing that God is Jehovah Jireh, my provider, left me with anxiety, worry, and fear when it came to providing for my small children. When it wasn't enough food to eat in the cabinets or not much to wear in the closet, I would take matters into my own hands by stealing food, clothes, or whatever else I felt we needed. I risked my freedom and a future with my children.

I will never forget the day I quickly realized that I wasn't about that life. I was hanging out with a well-known booster, aka a thief. According to Urban Dictionary, a booster is defined as, "A person who steals from retail stores only to then sell on the streets, usually for a discounted price."[2] Anyway, this young lady's family was known for stealing all types of high-end clothing. One day the young lady looked at me and said, "Why are you doing this? You smart; you got a future ahead of you. Me on the other hand, I'm a hoodrat. I have no choice but to do this!" A hoodrat is defined by Urban Dictionary as, "A person who lives and exhibits attitudes of

---

[2] Urban Dictionary, "booster,"
https://www.urbandictionary.com/define.php?term=booster.

inner-city life. Usually a negative connotation that implies poor upbringing, bad manners, little to no education and low class behavior."[3] God used this young lady, a former prisoner charged with grand theft, to help me see my worth. I wish she could've also seen her worth! Better yet, I wish I could've helped her see the value of her life as well.

During my boosting years, I also tried dating drug dealers to be a recipient of their riches and lifestyle. This phase lasted a lot longer than the boosting, and a lot longer than it should have. All of the riffraff and drama that came with that lifestyle was not for me. I grew tired of the lying, disrespectful, and cheating boyfriends. I was sick of fighting and dealing with drama from other girls. There was so much emotional and

---

[3] Urban Dictionary, "hoodrat," https://www.urbandictionary.com/define.php?term=Hoodrat.

physical abuse that came with dating guys that thought they were a god of some sort. There was also always the need to watch over my shoulder in fear of being robbed, killed, or arrested.

Unfortunately, that's how my life was when I lived without my Heavenly Father's guidance, instruction, peace, and comfort. It was readily available to me, but at that time, I chose my way, not His. I was in my early 20s, and sadly, a relationship with God was the furthest thing from my mind. God still watched over me and preserved me for such a time as this, but there were consequences to not being connected!

I have to thank God for His protection during those times and for being with me even when I didn't know that He was. I am thankful that God loved me too much to let me stay where I was and the way I was. I was lost, broken, wounded, hurt, angry, and frustrated.

These are all results of being a fatherless child biologically and prospectively.

My dad, whom I love dearly, came into my life when I was an infant. He and my mom eventually married, and then he joined the military. He was and still is very good to me. His strong work ethic, dedication, and sacrifice have always been a blessing. I never lacked love, joy, clothes, food, or shelter. We went on family vacations, had huge holidays, and most importantly, I was never abused, molested, or treated like a stepchild. I'm almost fifty years old, and to this day, I've never heard my dad refer to me as his stepdaughter. That is huge! I am forever grateful, but I must say that my gratitude was not always this solid. My preteen and teen years were tough. I suffered and struggled inside because I did not have a connection to my biological father. Then, things got worse for me after my biological father died when I was thirteen years old. I would later find out through extensive therapy that his death was an emotional turning point for me. I became very hurt and angry because there would never be a chance to connect with him—the man who created me.

Without knowing the root of my behavior, I started having sex, drinking alcohol, smoking marijuana, running away from home, disrespecting my parents, and so on. Some would say I was a fast tale teenage girl or that I was smelling myself. In all actuality, I was crying out for help. I was trying to fill the void created by my absentee biological father. The void grew after his death because I thought I was missing out on something.

This perspective and behavior continued for many years resulting in lifestyles, relationships, and a marriage that was not for me. Nothing changed in my mind or life until I allowed God to enter my heart and my mind. God's word and therapy helped me change my perspective. God's word transformed my mind, and I got rid of my stinkin' thinking.

I finally realized that God loved me so much that He gave me a biological father to give me life and a dad to get me through life! God always has a ram in the bush! Praise the Lord! God knew my biological father's lifestyle, and He knew that he would leave this earth early in life, so He gave me a dad to love me, provide for me, and guide me far beyond my biological father's life span. God knew exactly what I needed and exactly when to give it to me. I never lacked anything! It was a win-win situation! Thank you, Jesus!

Do you see how a fatherless deficit,

whether real or misconceived could lead to a road of destruction? I exaggerated the void with my stinkin' thinking, and I was looking for fulfillment in all the wrong places. Whatever your story is, please know that it is never too late for a happy ending. Be willing to put the work in to free yourself from childhood voids and issues. I encourage every fatherless child not to let your feelings for your earthly father to distort your feelings of the Heavenly Father. Trust me; there is no comparison!

Connect or reconnect with God today. He will lead you to heal and move forward in life. He will show you the areas of your heart that need work. He will even tell you the necessary steps to fix these issues. Maybe he's using that issue or that void in hopes that you'll cry out to him. You're waiting on God, but he's waiting for you! As Romans 12:2 says, let Him transform you by the renewing of your mind. Let Him change your perspective to see people and situations the way He sees them. He did it for me, and He'll do it for you . . . if you let Him.

REASON 2

GOD DESIRES FOR US TO BE IN A RELATIONSHIP WITH HIM

I'm hoping to effectively demonstrate and prove that God, Our Heavenly Father, wants a relationship with us. As I seek guidance for this particular task at hand, the lyrics to one of my favorite songs come to mind. Though many artists have sung the reckless love of God, the original artist is Corey Asbury. I would highly recommend you listen to the lyrics of this song before reading this chapter.

To me, these lyrics are a perfect description of God's desire to be in a relationship with us, and the song also details the depths that He'll go through to make this happen. When it comes to his children, God will not allow anything, anyone, or any place to get in His way. Praise the Lord for his love and power!

I find it so amazing that God (shepherd) will leave ninety-nine of His children (sheep) to search out one that's lost. They could be lost in an abusive relationship, addiction, depression, anxiety, suicidal thoughts, pride, or ego. It doesn't matter where we're lost. Thank God that He's bringing light into the situation and climbing mountains. Thank God that He'll reach down into the pit of hell to come after us! There is no place that He will not go to find His lost children.

He'll go to the psych ward, the crack house, my house, and to your house. He'll even go to a prison cell. It doesn't matter if you're in prison physically, emotionally, or mentally; He will come and pull His children out!

God will kick down the walls of hate, pride, racism, greed, unforgiveness, arrogance, and any other bondage that keeps you from being free in your mind, heart, and emotions. He will remove the lies that the enemy has tried to plant in our minds. As believers, we cannot allow ourselves to believe anything that is not aligned with God's word. The enemies' lies can make a person feel low or hopeless about a situation involving themselves or others. It's the enemies' job to lie, and the believer's responsibility to not believe the lie. This is done by searching the word of God to see what it says about the particular situation we're struggling with. How would you know what to dismiss as a lie if you don't know the truth? Brothers and sisters, we have to learn the word of God because it is our first line of defense against Satan's attack.

Please know that it's a lie from hell when you hear, you'll never get out of debt, you'll never find true love, your medical report is the end for you, your children will never turn away from their sinful lifestyles, and you'll never be successful. Anything that sounds like this is not from God. If these lies pop into your head, please rebuke them with the truth, aka, the word of

God. Do not allow things like this to take root in your mind. Allow God's word to immediately tear it down in Jesus's mighty name.

For example, when the enemy says you'll never be successful, a good response would be, "I rebuke you Satan. It is written in Jeremiah 29:11, that the Lord has plans to prosper me and not to harm me, but to give me a hope and a future. Thank you, Jesus, for the plans you have for me! Amen."

I've demonstrated through song that God desires a relationship with us. He will do whatever it takes to find us and to then love us into that place of wholeness, peace, and joy. Our heavenly Father does not desire for His children to be lost in this world. He wants us to be found, and He knows that He's the only one that can find us and bring us to that place of restoration in Him. Thank you, Jesus, for your reckless love!

Amen.

"Here I am! I stand at the door and knock. If anyone hears my voice and opens the door, I will come in and eat with that person, and they with me." Rev. 3:20 (NIV)

I find this scripture to be so amazing. It is the epitome of today's relationships. What is the main thing we do when we are either in a relationship with someone or building a relationship? We eat! We go out to dinner. We have dinner at the homes of family, friends, and co-workers. It is huge for Jesus to say that He'll come to our doors, knock, and if we let Him in, He will sit and fellowship with us over a meal! He didn't say, I'm coming to the door, and you better open it so we can eat. No! It's all based on us. He put the invitation out there to fellowship with us, and it's up to us to accept it. He's God and has the power to make us open the door. He could knock the door down, or He could threaten us and say that if we knew what was best, we'd open the door, but that's not how God is.

God is setting an example of how relationships should be. He is a gentleman that patiently waits to be allowed into our hearts, lives, and homes. He's not going to bang on the door or knock it down and force us to have dinner with him. What type of relationship would that be? Who would want to eat dinner with someone that forced them into it? I know I wouldn't. If it's not your heart's desire to be there with me to enjoy a good meal together, then I'm not interested. I only want to spend time with people who are willing and available. So, let's thank God for patiently waiting for us to let Him in.

The next scripture that I want to dig into regarding the topic of God's desire to be in a relationship with us, is John 15:13-17 (NIV) which says, "Greater love has no one than this: to lay down one's life for one's friends. You are my friends if you do what I command. I no longer call you servants, because a servant does not know his master's business. Instead, I have called you friends, for everything that I learned from my Father I have made known to you. You did not choose me, but I chose you and appointed you so that you might go and bear fruit—fruit that will last—and so that whatever you ask in my name the Father will give you. This is my command: Love each other."

The fact that Jesus laid down His life for us is astonishing! I mean this isn't something that is just normally and naturally done, especially in this day and age. How many of you have experienced suffering the consequences of someone else's wrongdoing? For instance, getting whoppings from your parents because of your sibling's bad behavior. I know I can relate, and I absolutely hated getting in trouble because of something my sisters did or did not do. In my opinion, everybody should suffer the consequences of their wrongdoing! Thank God that he sees things differently than I do! Praise God for sending us, Jesus!

Jesus's death was a supernatural act of obedience for the redemption of mankind. We were yet in sin, which made us enemies to God, but scripture says that Jesus laid down His life for His friends. Let's thank God that he sees us as friends, not enemies, nor sinners!

Well, one thing is for certain, Jesus had no sin. He was perfect and yet had to pay the ultimate price for the sins of mankind that should've allowed us to get our whoopings that we rightfully deserved. I am forever thankful for God's love, mercy, and grace. Amen.

So how does it make you feel knowing that it really should've been you and me on that cross? Knowing that Jesus died on the cross so that we wouldn't have to, should make us all feel beyond grateful, blessed, and humbled. We all should respect the sacrifice by honoring Jesus with our lives. Hallelujah to the King of Kings and Lord of Lords! Thank you, Jesus, for shedding your blood for me!

Once again, Jesus's death was the invitation to freedom from sin and a relationship with God for all eternity. He died so we could live a life of fullness with Him and the Heavenly Father. Will you accept His invitation today?

Many years ago, I chose to accept the invitation. I also opened the door and let Him in, and life could not be any better. I cannot lie and say my life has been a cakewalk since I've accepted Christ. I've encountered some very tough times! However, when I accepted Christ, His presence has been with me through every storm and struggle. So, with Christ, it's been plenteous in the midst of a drought, and it's been peaceful with hell going on all around me. I have joy even when I'm faced with sad and unwanted situations.

Matthew 11:28 (NIV) says, "Come to me all you who are weary and burdened, and I will give you rest."

Believe me when I say that this was my exact state when I accepted Christ. I was weary and burdened! I promise every one of you that over time I learned how to allow God to give me rest, no matter what's going on around me, within me, or being done to me. Everything is always good when I rest in him! He provided rest for me and He'll provide it for you if you let Him in.

Reason 3

Life is Better

When

You're

Connected

One day my co-worker and I were attempting to make copies of a few well needed documents. We pressed several different buttons on the copier, but we were not able to make any copies. We then looked around the machine to see what the problem could be. Then, someone yelled across the room, "That copier doesn't work. It's been broken for weeks!"

I replied, "Oh okay! Thank you; I didn't know that."

At that exact moment, my co-worker noticed the machine was unplugged. We both cracked up laughing, like well duh! Once she plugged it in, the screen lit up and we were good to go. What a difference something as simple as being plugged in makes. For us, it saved the trouble of having to look around for a working copier. For the copier, it was the difference of functioning in its purpose as opposed to being cast off as broken and of no use.

Apart from the power outlet, the copy machine was useless. There was absolutely nothing wrong with the machine. It had the ability to function just as it was created to, but without a power source, it sat there taking up space and collecting dust. Just think of all the jobs that the copier could've performed over the last several weeks that it remained unused. If someone had only noticed that it was unplugged!

Are you in a season where you are similar to the copy machine and need to be plugged in? Are you full of purpose but not connected to your source of power? Are you losing days, weeks, months, and years of purposeful work? If this is the case, please know that you were designed for something greater than sitting around taking up space and collecting dust. God created you with purpose. He has an area of influence waiting just for you, and He has work for you to do here on earth!

We all have a specific purpose and the only way to know that purpose and to fulfill that purpose is by staying connected to God. Knowing and fulfilling your purpose is one blessing that comes with your connection to God, but there are so many other blessings that come with staying connected to God. I've created a list of these blessings that I would like to share with my readers. I'm excited to share this list because I can personally testify that my life has been touched by each and every blessing listed below. I thank God for salvation, freedom, forgiveness, protection, deliverance, peace, healing, provision, grace, mercy, and joy. Thank you, Jesus! Now let's take a look at each of these blessings/gifts from God.

Salvation

Once an individual decides to answer the door and let God in, this is the beginning of salvation. Salvation in itself is an amazing gift from above, which also brings about many other gifts. It's like unwrapping one big gift box on Christmas morning, just to find a bunch of smaller gift boxes inside of that one big box. It's like the unwrapping never ends! As the scriptures below will illustrate, salvation is the prerequisite to receiving the gifts and promises of God such as forgiveness for your sins, the gift of the Holy Spirit, as well as the gift of eternal life.

"For it is by grace you have been saved, through faith—and this is not from yourselves, it is the gift of God—not by works, so that no one can boast." Eph. 2:8-9 (NIV)

Peter replied, "Repent and be baptized,

every one of you, in the name of Jesus Christ for the forgiveness of your sins. And you will receive the gift of the Holy Spirit." Acts 2:38 (NIV)

"For God so loved the world that he gave his one and only Son, that whoever believes in him shall not perish but have eternal life." John 3:16 (NIV)

Freedom/Forgiveness

Once a believer becomes saved, freedom from sin and forgiveness of sin go hand and hand. They are both amazing gifts from God. Once we confess that Christ is our personal Lord and Savior He imparts the Holy Spirit within us to guide us and lead us into a lifestyle free of sin. A lifestyle that consists of new mindsets and habits. Not saying that we become perfect and will have no sin; that's far from the case. Once we confess

Christ as our Lord and Savior and confess our sin, we are no longer slaves to sin. We no longer find pleasure in our old sinful ways. Sin starts to loosen its grip on us as we aim to be pleasing in the Lord's eyes. The blood of Jesus Christ cleanses us and purifies us from past, present, and future sins. These are sins that God forgives and remembers no more. Thank you, Jesus!

"For the grace of God has appeared that offers Salvation to all people. It teaches us to say "No" to ungodliness and worldly passions, and to live a self-controlled, upright and godly lives in this present age." Titus 2:11-12 (NIV)

"But now that you have been set free from sin and have become slaves of God, the benefit you reap leads to holiness, and the result is eternal life." Rom. 6:22 (NIV)

"But if we walk in the light as He is in the light, we have fellowship with one another, and the blood of Jesus Christ His Son cleanses us from all sin. If we say that we have no sin, we deceive ourselves, and the truth is not in us. If we confess our sins, He is faithful and just to forgive us our sins and to cleanse us from all unrighteousness." 1 John 1:7-9 (NKJV)

Protection

God protects His children from harm, death, destruction, bad decisions, and distractions that are disguised as people, places, and things. At times, He has to even protect us from ourselves. When I think of the Lord's protection, one scripture automatically comes to mind. Psalm 91 is the ultimate prayer of protection. This particular Psalm covers every ground when it comes to God's awesome power and ability to protect His children.

Psalm 91 lays out the fact that children of God are protected from present dangers, plots, and plans of the enemy. We are protected from various harm, plagues, disease, and traps of sin. Morning, noon, or night, we are safe under the shadow of the Almighty. Disease, danger, death, and destruction could be going on all around us, but it will not come near us. The Lord's outstretched arms will cover us with His feathers, and His angels will serve and protect us daily.

Psalm 91 reminds us that when a believer continually seeks His presence, they are not only safe but also have the authority and power to walk all over Satan and his army. Lastly, there will be times when God allows trouble in the life of a believer, but we have the privilege of crying out to him. When we cry out, we can have confidence in knowing that God hears and delivers us. If you are facing trouble or just want peace in knowing that you're protected, please let Psalm 91 be your prayer today.

"Whoever dwells in the shelter of the Most High will rest in the shadow of the Almighty. I will say of the LORD, 'He is my refuge and my fortress, my God, in whom will I trust." Surely he will save you from the fowler's snare and from the deadly pestilence. He will cover you with his feathers, and under his wings you will find refuge; his faithfulness will be your shield and rampart. You will not fear the terror of night, nor the arrow that flies by day, nor the pestilence that stalks in the darkness, nor the plague that destroys at midday. A thousand may fall at your side, ten thousand at your right hand, but it will not come near you. You will only observe with your eyes and see the punishment of the wicked. If you say, "The LORD is my refuge," and you make the Most High your dwelling, no harm will overtake you, no disaster will come near your tent. For he will command his angels concerning you to guard you in all your ways; they will lift you up in their hands, so that you will not strike your foot against a stone. You will tread on the lion and the cobra; you will trample the great lion and the serpent. 'Because he loves me,' says the LORD, 'I will rescue him; I will protect him, for he acknowledges my name. He will call on me, and I will answer him; I will be with him in trouble, I will deliver him and honor him. With long life I will satisfy him and show him my salvation.'" Ps. 91:1-16 (NIV)

Deliverance

Scripture tells us that as believers we can depend on our Heavenly Father to deliver us from ALL trouble. There is not any form of trouble that we cannot get delivered from. As we seek God and surrender our lives to His will and His ways, He then begins to do a new thing in our lives. He delivers us from the people, places, and things that have us in bondage. Old habits, hindering mindsets, bad relationships, and destructive lifestyles must cease once God equips us with wisdom, direction, strength, and power. As we seek God, He shows us the things we need to work on, and where we need deliverance. What do you need deliverance from today? Remember that God delivers us from ALL trouble; He is not limited! He delivers us from abuse, addiction, fear, anxiety, worry, unemployment, depression, sickness, financial distress, troubled marriages, hate, bitterness, unforgiveness, evil traps, and the plans of others. Thank you, Lord, for deliverance!

No matter what your trouble is today, if

you are a believer, you can cry out for help, strength, and answers. God will hear your sincere prayer and deliver you! Please receive your deliverance today in Jesus's mighty name! Amen.

"The righteous cry out, and the Lord hears them; he delivers them from all their troubles." Ps. 34:17 (NIV)

"Submit yourselves, then, to God. Resist the devil, and he will flee from you." James 4:7 (NIV)

"But forget all that—it is nothing compared to what I am going to do. For I am about to do something new. See, I have already begun! Do you not see it? I will make a pathway through the wilderness. I will create rivers in the dry wasteland." Isa. 43:18-19 (NLT)

Peace

It is something about saying or seeing the word peace that makes my heart smile. I am so very thankful for all the beautiful gifts that the Lord bestows upon His children. Every single one of His gifts is to be appreciated and cherished. Where would we be without salvation, freedom, forgiveness, protection, deliverance, peace, healing, provision, grace, mercy, and joy? The list of blessings goes on and on. These are just a few that I chose to highlight in this particular book. The truth is that we would be resting in our graves, or sitting in our miserable mess if it had not been for God pouring out His love and His generous gifts. Thank you, Jesus, for your continued generosity!

I must say that out of all the gifts that I've mentioned above, peace is the most pleasurable to me. I enjoy them all, but peace just touches me in a place that I cannot describe. It's kind of hard to explain, so allow me to take a moment to define peace.

Your Dictionary defines peace as, "A calmness and tranquility, a time when there are no wars going on or the state of having no war or conflict."[4]

What I love about peace is the calmness and the absence of war and conflict. Even if there is something going on around me, I still have a peace that surpasses all understanding.

I feel closer to God in my times of calmness and tranquility. It feels like God is literally beside me keeping me company. All the other gifts show me that God loves me and blessed me with something. With peace, it's like I have Him right here. He's the gift that I personally get to experience and feel.

---

[4] Your Dictionary, "peace," https://www.yourdictionary.com/peace.

"Peace I leave with you; my peace I give you. I do not give to you as the world gives. Do not let your hearts be troubled and do not be afraid." John 14:27 (NIV)

"These things I have spoken to you, that in Me you may have peace. In the world you will have tribulation, but be of good cheer, I have overcome the world." John 16:33 (NKJV)

"You will keep in perfect peace those whose minds are steadfast, because they trust in you." Isa. 26:3 (NIV)

"Be anxious for nothing, but in everything by prayer and supplication, with thanksgiving, let your request be made known to God; and the peace of God, which surpasses all understanding, will guard your hearts and minds through Christ

Jesus." Phil. 4:6-7 (NKJV)

Healing

Children of God can boldly expect and receive healing! It is written in Exodus 23:25 that God will take sickness away from us. Whether it's being healed from a broken heart, the common cold, coronavirus, or cancer, please know that God is willing and ready to bless you with the gift of healing. Matthew 21:22 says that if you believe, you will receive whatever you ask for in prayer. God is not limited to a specific type of ailment; He can heal you physically, emotionally, mentally, and spiritually. It doesn't matter how long you've dealt with the issue; please don't lose hope, and never stop believing the word of God.

In Mark 5:25-34, there was a woman that suffered from constant bleeding for twelve years. She went to several doctors spending all she had but was never healed. Things actually appeared as if she was getting worse.

Can you imagine being sick for years and paying totally out of pocket or paying a bunch of copays? Most of us Christian folks would've lost hope or perhaps gotten angry with God for the prolonged illness.

The woman with the issue of blood was faithful to believe everything that she had heard about Jesus. She knew He was coming to town and that her healing could only come from Him. She thought, "If I can just touch his robe; I will be healed."

Brothers and sisters, she didn't say if she could touch Him or ask for healing. She said if she could simply touch His robe! She touched the robe and the bleeding stopped. She was instantly healed!

Then Jesus said to her "Daughter, your faith has made you well. Go in peace. Your suffering is over." Mark 5:34 (NLT)

According to Acts 10:34, God is not a respecter of persons. In other words, He does not show favoritism. He healed the woman with the issue of blood and He'll do it for you too!

"But I will restore you to health and heal your wounds, declares the Lord." Jer. 30:17 (NIV)

"He heals the brokenhearted and binds up their wounds." Ps. 147:3 (NIV)

"And the people all tried to touch him, because power was coming from him and healing them all." Luke 6:19 (NIV)

Provision

God's provision has no limits. Each day we are blessed to be recipients of His provision.

From the air that we breathe, the food that we taste, the opening of our eyes in the morning, the clothes that we have, the jobs that we get to work, the cars we drive, the sermons that we are able to hear, the creativity and ideas that come to our mind, the strength and energy that carries us through the day, and the houses that we live in. God has granted us comfort and strength during grief. The Lord has allowed many of us to survive this deadly global pandemic and kept us financially afloat during the struggling economy. God has provided us with faith and hope during tough times, and protection during times of racial injustice and police brutality. He has given us wisdom, direction, courage, guidance, strength, and discernment in the midst of making difficult decisions. Because of God, we have legs to walk in the park, and hands to hold our babies. We are able to make it home safely after a long day at work. Our bills are paid on time. We have the love of family and friends. Many of us have health insurance, healthy children, strong marriages, and successful businesses.

The list goes on and on. The fact is that God is always providing for His people in many ways. Sometimes it's seen and sometimes it is not. We have no idea of the things that God has provided for us behind the scenes. He is always working on our behalf. Sometimes it's small things, and at other times, we experience miracles, signs, and wonders. Then, there are those times that God's provision is right in front of us, but we miss it because it didn't come in the package that we were expecting. Please make room for God to be God! Take the limits off of Him. He's a BIG God, and He does BIG things! "Exceedingly, abundantly, above all we ask or think." Eph. 3:20 (NKJV)

He knows exactly what He is doing. We don't know what He knows and we don't see what He sees. We must believe that He is working on our behalf by giving us what we need, how we need it, and when we need it. Amen.

"The Lord is my shepherd, I lack nothing." Ps. 23:1 (NIV)

"The lions may grow weak and hungry, but those who seek the Lord lack no good thing." Ps. 34:10 (NIV)

"If you then, who are evil, know how to give good gifts to your children, how much more will your Father who is in Heaven give good things to those who ask him!" Matt. 7:11 (ESV)

Grace/Mercy

These two are very similar in meaning but are very different. If we are not careful, we can easily confuse the two. Simply put, grace is the unmerited favor of God that goes beyond mercy. Grace is God blessing us with divine kindness and compassion, despite the fact that we don't deserve it. Grace is also God giving us the ability to do something that is humanly impossible on our own.

Mercy is God withholding the judgment or punishment that we deserved for something we did wrong.

For further understanding, let's look at Grace/Mercy from the lens of a parent.

You arrive at parent teacher's conference, and your eighth-grade child gets a terrible report from the teacher. Their grades have dropped and their behavior has been out of control lately. There's no apparent explanation of what's going on with the child. Things are going well at home. The teacher seems to believe that the recent decline in grades and behavior is due to the child just trying to fit in with the wrong crowd. In your mind, you're thinking that you're going to "lay hands" on your child once you get home. Instead, you extend grace and mercy by just talking to them once you get home. The kid deserved to be punished in some way, but because of your compassion and loving kindness (grace), they didn't receive punishment. The punishment was withheld (mercy).

Now for the believer, Jesus's outstretched arms on the cross and the salvation that came with it, is what grace and mercy look like for us. When Jesus took our place on the cross, our Heavenly Father extended compassion and loving-kindness by withholding the punishment that we deserved. We deserved that punishment, not Jesus! Thank you, Lord, for allowing us to continually experience your grace and mercy! Thank you, Father, for not treating us as our sins deserve. Thank you, Father, for not repaying us according to our iniquities. Ps. 103:10 (NIV)

Help us Lord to also extend grace and mercy to others, as your word says, "Blessed are the merciful, for they shall obtain mercy." Matt. 5:7 (KJV)

"But by the grace of God I am what I am, and his grace to me was not without effect. No, I worked harder than all of them—yet not I, but the grace of God that was with me."
1 Cor. 15:10 (NIV)

"Let us then approach God's throne of grace with confidence, so that we may receive mercy and find grace to help us in our time of need." Heb. 4:16 (NIV)

"He saved us, not because of righteous things we had done, but because of his mercy. He saved us through the washing of rebirth and renewal by the Holy Spirit." Titus 3:5 (NIV)

Joy

Lexico defines joy as, "A feeling of great pleasure and happiness."[5]

The article, "What is Joy in Christianity?" describes joy as, "Choosing to respond to external circumstances with inner contentment and satisfaction."[6]

Believers don't have to wait until something good happens in order to feel good or

---

[5] Lexico, "joy," https://www.lexico.com/definition/joy.
[6] Walker, Mel, "What is Joy in Christianity?" https://www.christianity.com/wiki/christian-terms/what-is-joy-in-christianity.html.

satisfied, that's called happiness. Happiness is a fleeting emotion based on circumstances. When circumstances are positive, happiness results. When circumstances are unfavorable, happiness disappears. Overall, happiness is a wonderful feeling to experience, but believers have access to joy. Joy is something greater. Joy is everlasting! Joy is not based on what is going on around us; it goes beyond that. Joy is internal; it comes from the Holy Spirit that lives inside of us. If you are a believer, joy is a by-product of the Holy Spirit that comes from God. Joy is openly available for every believer to receive, but you have to choose to accept it and walk in it.

It is possible to have true joy in the midst of undesired circumstances. No matter what is going on around us, believers can count it all joy when we are met with various trials. James 1:2 This is not saying that you are joyful about what's going on, but that you can choose to be joyful about the ending results. You choose joy by knowing that God is in control of your life and situations. It says in 1 Peter 5:7 that when you truly trust God, you can cast your concerns upon Him and live in contentment knowing that He is working on your behalf. Trusting and believing God is what activates true joy in your heart.

"But the fruit of the Spirit is love, joy, peace, forbearance, kindness, goodness, faithfulness." Gal. 5:22 (NIV)

"For the kingdom of God is not a matter of eating and drinking, but of righteousness, peace and joy in the Holy Spirit." Rom. 14:17 (NIV)

"These things I have spoken to you, that my joy may be in you, and that your joy may be full." John 15:11 (ESV)

Praise God for His faithfulness! Praise Him for His many blessings that are seen and unseen. He's the king of kings and Lord of lords. What an honor and privilege it is to have Him as our Heavenly Father. We should not take this lightly. As children of God, we must put our work in. Every fruitful relationship requires both parties to be actively involved, faithful, and committed. We cannot expect God to do all the work. Yes, He is all-powerful and can do anything, but what type of relationship would that be if He was the only one putting in work? Let's show God that we are fully committed to doing our part to *Stay Connected* to Him.

As Disciples of Christ, we must discipline ourselves so that we can become more like Christ. More of Him and less of us! The only way a person's character rubs off on us is by spending time with them. The more time we spend hanging out with someone, the more we start behaving like them, talking like them, and sometimes even thinking like them. With that being said, if our goal is to be more like Christ, then we must *Stay Connected* to Him. In other words, we have to hang out with Him. Therefore, let's go over seven simple disciplines that will allow us to do exactly that.

Seven

Simple Disciplines

Go to Church

Believers should be connected to a bible preaching and teaching church. Church is where we gather with other believers to fellowship, strengthen, and sharpen one another through prayer, praise, and worship. Church is where we welcome the spiritually sick and wounded. We welcome them in with open arms and restore them back to spiritual health. This is where we learn about God and His word. This is where we use our spiritual gifts and talents to advance the kingdom of God. Can we show God some love by visiting Him at His house? We visit everybody else. Most of us have a weekly routine to visit our parents, children, friends, siblings, etc. Why not make God's house a weekly priority?

If you are reading this and your heart is one that is against corporate worship, please know that this is not God's will for you. I'm sorry if you've had a bad experience within the church that may have turned your heart cold towards corporate worship. If this is the case, maybe God is saying that this is the time to pray, receive healing, and deliverance in this area.

"For where two or three gather in my name, there am I with them." Matt. 18:20 (NIV)

"I was glad when they said unto me, let us go into the house of the Lord." Ps. 122:1 (KJV)

Prioritize Your Day

Most of us have very busy lives. We're busy working, going to school, taking care of our families, running businesses, overseeing ministries, exercising, etc. Sometimes we can become too busy and push ourselves to the limit. If we are not careful, busyness can lead to physical, mental, emotional, and spiritual exhaustion. This is not God's desire for us. He desires for our lives to not just be busy, but to be fruitful. So, in order for our labor to produce fruit, we want to be busy doing the right things; the things that God has for us to do. The only way to ensure that we are doing the right things at the right time is by spending quiet time with God every day! Make this your priority! This is the only way to hear from God for clarity, direction, and guidance. The quiet time with God is the time that we should be praying, reading our bibles, and having daily devotional. We should spend this time praising and worshipping God with or without some good gospel music playing to get things stirred up. We have to set the atmosphere for God to show up!

Create a secret place to go at an appointed time of day to be in the presence of God. This can be in your bedroom, at the kitchen table, in the shower, or your car. It doesn't matter where or when; just start making time with God a habit in your daily lives. Everybody has different schedules and routines, so you have to find out what works best for you.

For me, it is easier to spend quiet time with the Lord first thing in the morning as stated in Psalm 63:1. I love to wake up early and experience being in His presence. I want God to be the first person I encounter and speak to in the morning. This interaction sets the tone for my whole day. And believe me, there is a big difference in my day when I rush out before spending time with God. Something just feels off and it always seems like those days aren't as awesome as the others.

"He says, 'Be still, and know that I am God; I will be exalted among the nations, I will be exalted in the earth.'" Ps. 46:10 (NIV)

"But when you pray, go into your room, close the door and pray to your Father, who is unseen. Then your Father, who sees what is done in secret, will reward you." Matt. 6:6 (NIV)

Give

We can also stay connected to God by sharing what we have with others. God loves a generous and cheerful giver. Giving should be done from the heart and not for attention or reward. There are many ways to give. We should give to our local church and organizations that are doing good things for the community. We should always give to those that are in need such as family, friends, strangers, the hungry, and the homeless. When we give to others, it's as if we are giving to God himself. We are God's hands and feet on earth working on His behalf. Therefore, we have to always be on the lookout for ways to bless others. A believer's prayer should be for God to lead them to the people and the places that need them.

"A generous person will prosper; whoever refreshes others will be refreshed." Prov. 11:25 (NIV)

"Give, and it will be given to you. A good measure, pressed down, shaken together and running over, will be poured into your lap. For with the measure you use, it will be measured to you." Luke 6:38 (NIV)

"Each of you should give what you have decided in your heart to give, not reluctantly or under compulsion, for God loves a cheerful giver." 2 Cor. 9:7 (NIV)

Serve

"Not so with you. Instead, whoever wants to become great among you must be your servant, and whoever wants to be first must be slave of all. For even the Son of Man did not come to be served, but to serve, and to give life as a ransom for many." Mark 10:43-45 (NIV)

Jesus came down from heaven to be a perfect example of what servanthood looks like. Everywhere He went, He was a blessing to someone, and He walked from town to town to fulfill the needs of others. He washed the feet of His disciples, and He laid down His life for all sinners. He humbly put others first. He wasn't concerned about His own needs. Jesus knew that as He took care of others, His Father would take care of Him.

This is how our ministry should look. Ministry goes beyond Sunday morning worship in the church house. We have to put ourselves and anything we are facing to the side and get out in the world to serve others. We must always seek opportunities to meet the needs of others with our gifts, talents, and abilities. This can be done in and outside of the church. Perhaps you have a great singing voice which could be used in the choir. Maybe you're off from work on Fridays; this could be a great time to volunteer in your community.

There are numerous ways to serve others. You just need to find something that fits you. I love serving others in my church and the homeless population. Serving brings me so much joy and comfort. I found that it's just as much a blessing for the giver as it is for the recipient. Diligently serving others allowed me to maneuver through a hurtful divorce with joy still in my heart and a smile on my face. Let's be more like Jesus and serve somebody today!

"Serve wholeheartedly, as if you were serving the Lord, not people." Ephesians 6:7 NIV

"Let your light so shine before men, that they may see your good works and glorify your Father in heaven." Matt. 5:16 (NKJV)

Pray

I know that I previously mentioned prayer as being part of our quiet time with The Lord. However, prayer is such a huge part of a believer's life, so I wanted to take a little more time to focus on this topic. Prayer is a necessity that is vital to the believer. It is how we communicate with God. We lay our request out before God and patiently await His answer. We also give thanks and praises unto God during our prayer time. Prayer is also a time to clear our minds and hearts before God. Sometimes you just need a listening ear to get some things off your chest without expecting anything in return.

Prayer is a huge defense method to use against the enemy, especially when we are praying the scriptures. Praying the word of God makes our prayers more powerful. When we speak and pray the scriptures, we are coming into agreement with God. When we are in agreement with God, His power is then released to answer our prayers. So, for instance, if you are experiencing financial struggles, you should seek out scriptures that apply to finances, peace, and faith. This will cover all areas of that one particular struggle. After you find the scriptures, then write them down. Speak these scriptures over you and your finances during your prayer time. In doing this, you are "reminding" God of what He promised. God is not a man, so He does not lie! Num. 23:19 (NLT) Therefore, He will show up and show out in your situation, in his time, and in his way!

Prayer is **NOT** a time to beg, whine, or complain. As believers, we know that God hears us when we seek Him with our whole heart and are in a relationship with Him. We can be confident in His word, and in His power! Therefore, there is no need to beg or to feel hopeless about your situation. If you are not confident in God, then you are not spending enough time with God or in His word. I mean it would be kind of hard to have confidence in a stranger. If this is where you stand today, you need to spend more time with God in order to know Him for yourself. You do this by making it a priority to read His word. His word is living and powerful and is full of many promises that will encourage and strengthen you. Tell God that you want to get closer to Him today, and ask Him to show you how.

Also, prayer is not a time to only ask for things. Who would want to hear from someone every day and all they do is ask for stuff? Not me, and not God! That would show clear signs of being immature, rude, selfish, ungrateful, and inconsiderate. Let's not take our prayer time lightly or for granted. We as believers are truly blessed to have the opportunity to approach the throne of God, and it doesn't stop there! According to Hebrews 4:16, we can approach the throne boldly, and be confident that our prayer is heard in Jesus's mighty name.

There are so many amazing scriptures about prayer. Listed below are some of my favorites. I pray that they fill you with hope, peace, strength, and encouragement.

"This, then, is how you should pray: Our

Father in heaven, hallowed be your name, your kingdom come, your will be done, on earth as it is in heaven. Give us today our daily bread. And forgive us our debts, as we also have forgiven our debtors. And lead us not into temptation, but deliver us from the evil one." Matt. 6:9-13 (NIV)

"Do not be anxious about anything, but in every situation, by prayer and petition, with thanksgiving, present your request to God." Phil. 4:6 (NIV)

"I call on you, my God, for you will answer me; turn your ear to me and hear my prayer." Ps. 17:6 (NIV)

"You will pray to him, and he will hear you, and you will fulfill your vows." Job 22:27 (NIV)

"Is anyone among you in trouble? Let them pray. Is anyone happy? Let them sing songs of praise." James 5:13 (NIV)

"Therefore I tell you, whatever you ask in prayer, believe that you have received it, and it will be yours." Mark 11:24 (ESV)

"Then you will call on me and come and pray to me, and I will listen to you." Jer. 29:12 (NIV)

"If you believe, you will receive whatever you ask for in prayer." Matt. 21:22 (NIV)

"If my people, who are called by my name, will humble themselves and pray and seek my face and turn from their wicked ways, then I will hear from heaven, and I will forgive their sin and will heal their land." 2 Chron. 7:14 (NIV)

"Never stop praying." 1 Thess. 5:17 (NLT)

Be Obedient

"See, I am setting before you today a blessing and a curse—the blessing if you obey the commands of the LORD your God that I am giving you today; the curse if you disobey the commands of the LORD your God and turn from the way that I command you today by following other gods, which you have not known." Deut. 11:26-28 (NIV)

The scripture above clearly states that blessings come from being obedient. The entire bible is full of many miracles that followed someone's obedience to the Lord's instructions. In Luke 5:1-11, Peter and his fishing partners were instructed by Jesus to put their nets in a certain location to catch fish. Peter had been fishing all day and hadn't caught anything, but his words to Jesus were, "Master, we've worked hard all night and haven't caught anything. But because you say so, I will let down the nets." Luke

5:5 (NIV)

When Peter and the other fishermen followed Jesus's instructions, they caught tons of fish. They caught so many fish that their nets broke. Peter and his partners were so amazed by this. The miracle that they witnessed led them to be a disciple of Christ. Jesus told them that they will now fish for people, and they then left everything and followed Jesus.

Peter and his friends never would've experienced the fishing miracle, and they probably would've never become disciples if Peter wouldn't have been obedient to Jesus's instructions. Peter could've easily said, "Look Master, I'm tired, thanks for the advice but I'm done for the day!" but instead, He responded in obedience and witnessed a miracle. This proves that miracles follow obedience!

Then, in John 2:1-11, the famous turning

water into wine miracle happened because of obedience. Once the wine ran out at the wedding, Jesus's mother Mary told Him about it and she told the servants to do whatever Jesus instructed. After Jesus briefly questioned His mother, Jesus told the servants to fill the waterpots with water. Once they filled them to the brim, He told them to take some out now and take over to the master of the feast. They did all that they were told. When the master tasted the water, it had turned into wine! Miraculous! This would've never happened if the servants would've questioned Jesus by saying, "What the heck are we doing this for? They need wine, not water!" The miracle probably wouldn't have happened if they would've procrastinated. They operated in Jesus's timing. He said do it now, and that's what they did!

This is what obedience should look like for

a believer. When we get a word from God, we follow it. We are to follow the word of God and personalized instructions that He gives each of us whether it makes sense or not! Usually, it will not make sense to our natural minds because Jesus operates in the supernatural which is beyond our ability to comprehend. So, please don't get caught up on everything making sense. If you do, you just might miss out on your blessing.

Also, don't get thrown off by downplaying the smaller things. I don't care if it's something as simple as calling to check on a loved one. If He puts it on your heart to do it, then you should do it. If you wait, it could be too late. Maybe that person is in need of something, or maybe that person is about to pass away and that will be your opportunity to talk to them before they pass on. We never know why God is telling us to do something. Our job is to respond in obedience.

Do whatever He says, when He says it, and the way He says it! There is a grace period for everything, but remember that delayed obedience is still disobedience, and we don't want to live in disobedience.

When we are obedient to God's word and His instruction, we show Him that we not only trust Him but that we also love and respect Him. When you love and respect someone, you aim to please them. So, let's aim to please God today by walking in obedience. As scripture shows, obedience brings about blessings. We all need the blessings of God in every area of our lives! Amen.

"Jesus replied, 'Anyone who loves me will obey my teaching. My Father will love them, and we will come to them and make our home with them.'" John 14:23 (NIV)

"Walk in obedience to all that the Lord your God has commanded you, so that you may live and prosper and prolong your days in the land that you will possess." Deut. 5:33 (NIV)

"If you are willing and obedient, you shall eat the good of the land." Isa. 1:19 (ESV)

"Why do you call me 'Lord, Lord', and not do what I tell you?" Luke 6:46 (ESV)

"But he said, 'Blessed rather are those who hear the word of God and keep it!'" Luke 11:28 (ESV)

Be Thankful

"Give thanks in all circumstances; for this is the will of God in Christ Jesus for you." 1 Thess. 5:18 (ESV)

No matter what is going on with us or around us, there is always something to be thankful for. 1 Thessalonians 5:18 states to give thanks in ALL circumstances. It does not say give thanks in the good circumstances, or when everything is pleasing and going your way. All circumstances mean the good, the bad, and the ugly. Through it all, we must find something to be thankful to God about.

The fact that you are still alive is a great start. It means that God has kept you alive for a reason. He has not counted you out! So, don't count Him out! Take inventory and instead of focusing on everything that is wrong, change your perspective and focus on everything that is going right. Once you've taken inventory then give thanks unto the Lord. Thank Him for everything that you have. Thank Him for everything that you are and are not. Thank God that you are **NOT** sick in your mind or body today. If you are sick in your mind or body then thank Him for medicine, medical professionals, and counselors. Thank Him for His word that says, "By his stripes, you are healed." 1 Peter 2:24 (KJV)

If you are having problems with your finances, be thankful, because according to Philippians 4:19, you serve a God that will supply all of your needs. Even though you may be having financial troubles, you still have many other things to be thankful for. Give God thanks for what you do have!

Whatever you may be going through today, please don't allow it to rob you of being thankful. Think about it for a second, how would you feel if you've given someone several gifts and they didn't say thank you because you have yet to give them the one gift that they really want? You wouldn't be very pleased with their ungrateful behavior and you probably wouldn't give them that gift after all, even though you were secretly working behind the scenes to provide it to them.

Well, that's how it works with the kingdom of God. Our Heavenly Father blesses us with so much, and we don't give Him the thanks He deserves because we focus our attention on the one or two areas in our lives that are challenging. Why should He continuously bless us if we are going to be ungrateful? Let's not block our blessings. One of the keys to being blessed is to be thankful. So, let's give thanks unto the Lord, for He is good!

"Enter his gates with thanksgiving, and his courts with praise; give thanks to him and praise his name." Ps. 100:4 (NIV)

"Oh give thanks to the Lord, for he is good, for his steadfast love endures forever!" Ps. 107:1 (ESV)

"Giving thanks always and for everything to God the Father in the name of our Lord Jesus Christ." Eph. 5:20 (ESV)

Staying connected to God is critical for the life of a believer. God has a plan for each of His children, and in order to walk into the fullness of His plans, one must seek Him daily. God's plans and purposes will not fully manifest in our lives if we live life on our terms. It is not enough to simply believe in the name of the Lord. It is time to get serious about our salvation.

God created us to be in a relationship with Him. He desires this, and life is so much better when we give God what He desires. A life lived with God, is a life filled with many blessings.

STAY CONNECTED

We become recipients of salvation, freedom, forgiveness, protection, deliverance, peace, healing, grace, mercy, and joy. Let's not take God's plans, purposes, and promises for granted. As stated in John 10:10, He came to give us life and life more abundantly, so choose God today! Say yes to His will and His ways! Say yes to making Him a habit! Say yes to staying connected!

Father God, I come to you today on behalf of every one of my readers. Lord, we say thank you for your reckless love. We thank you for being a good good Father! Help us Lord, to be more grateful for you and the good gifts that you give us. Thank you, Lord, that we can trust you and cast all our cares upon you, Lord. Thank you for the perfect plans that you have for all of us. Help us Father, to walk with you in this life. Help us Lord, to make you a priority. Help us Lord, to put away the people, places, and things that distract us from getting to know you better. We need more time to read and to pray, so show us how to do this, Lord! Help us Lord, to make more time to serve others. Help us Lord, to be cheerful givers. Help us Lord, to be more loving by showing grace and mercy to others. Lord, help us to be more like you today. Help us Lord, to be obedient to you today in all our ways. Lord, we need you; we love you. Lord, we want you today! Help us to fulfill the desires of your heart today. Help us to position ourselves today so we can receive all that you have for us, and all that you have for us to do today. In the mighty name of Jesus, I pray. So, it is done. Amen! Amen! And Amen!

www.ingramcontent.com/pod-product-compliance
Lightning Source LLC
LaVergne TN
LVHW020935090426
835512LV00020B/3365